T0144048

Adoption Affirmations

Fulfilling Your Family Tree

Keri Gee Semmelman
and
Nikki Biers

Adoption Affirmations

Resourceful guidance,
visual inspiration,
and loving support
to help you,
Adoptive Parents-to-be,
through your journey
of creating or expanding
your own precious
family tree.

Written by
Keri Gee Semmelman
and
Nikki Biers

Flipbook Illustrations by
Cheron Bartee

Copyright © 2018 Keri Gee Semmelman and Nikki Biers.

All rights reserved. No part of this book may be used or reproduced by any means, graphic, electronic, or mechanical, including photocopying, recording, taping or by any information storage retrieval system without the written permission of the author except in the case of brief quotations embodied in critical articles and reviews.

Flipbook Illustrations by
Cheron Bartee

Edited by
Eve Gumpel, Good Writing Matters

This book is a work of nonfiction. Unless otherwise noted, the author and the publisher make no explicit guarantees as to the accuracy of the information contained in this book.

Balboa Press books may be ordered through booksellers or by contacting:

Balboa Press
A Division of Hay House
1663 Liberty Drive
Bloomington, IN 47403
www.balboapress.com
1 (877) 407-4847

Because of the dynamic nature of the Internet, any web addresses or links contained in this book may have changed since publication and may no longer be valid. The views expressed in this work are solely those of the author and do not necessarily reflect the views of the publisher, and the publisher hereby disclaims any responsibility for them.

ISBN: 978-1-9822-1254-4 (sc)
ISBN: 978-1-9822-1255-1 (e)

Library of Congress Control Number: 2018911190

Print information available on the last page.

Balboa Press rev. date: 10/31/2018

BALBOA.
PRESS
A DIVISION OF HAY HOUSE

Dedication

We dedicate this book to every person who has
. . . dreamed of adopting.
. . . endured numerous heartbreaks during his or her adoption journey yet never gave up hope.
. . . been blessed to adopt.

To every courageous person who has given a baby up for adoption in order to give the child a better future.

To every adopted child. You are the most treasured gift an adoptive parent could ever hope for.

To our precious adopted children who fulfilled our family trees.

To our own helpful circles of support, especially our husbands Elliot and Michael, who have made our dreams of becoming adoptive moms a breathtaking reality.

And in memory of our own parents and grandparents, who loved us and taught us well.

Forever Grateful . . . Forever Moms,
~ *Keri Gee and Nikki*

For more about Adoption Affirmations
go to: www.adoptionaffirmations.com

Contents

Introduction

Pursuing adoption takes enormous courage, strength, and love, and also a tremendous amount of self-awareness. Staying positive, hopeful, and patient is necessary. The minute you make the decision to adopt . . . your becoming a parent is real. And, the minute you make that decision, the "self-talk" begins. One day you may feel completely hopeful and excited, another day possibly disillusioned and even wanting to give up on your journey to adopt. Throughout what we call your "emotional pregnancy," you'll find that what you say to yourself and also what you hear from others—especially during the tough times—can make all the difference in your becoming an adoptive parent.

The nearly 80 affirmations within these pages along with the visual inspiration of the growing family tree are to help you talk with yourself in productive ways so you remain hopeful, confront your fears with grace, feel in control during the highs and lows, and increase your joy during your journey to adopt.

Between us, we've gone through nearly every twist and turn one can experience during the journey, and we also know the joy of adopting. Through it all, we definitely learned what to say and not say to ourselves to keep our hearts open and arms ready to embrace every child who came our way. May these affirmations help you do the same.

How to Use Your Book

These affirmations are for every part of the journey you encounter—from making the decision to adopt, ensuring you have a good support system of loved ones and adoption professionals, meeting the birth mom and the child, enduring failed adoptions (if that happens), and ultimately becoming an adoptive parent. The affirmations are organized chronologically, starting with your decision to adopt and ending with tender words from your baby/child-to-be. In some sections you'll find many affirmations to choose from, in others you'll find just a few because they say everything you need to tell yourself.

To make the most of this book, you'll want to refer to it both proactively and reactively. For example, if you are about to meet a birth mom for the first time, you'll want to read the section about preparing to meet the birth mom prior to doing so. Or, if an adoption has fallen through, you can immediately strengthen yourself by reading the affirmations dealing with failed adoptions.

Read each affirmation out loud. Let the words sink in. Feel them, believe them, and embrace them. While we hope every affirmation resonates with you, we encourage you to pick those that really speak to you so that you can sincerely speak to yourself. You may want to highlight those you are drawn to so you can easily find them daily and whenever needed. There may be times that you'll instead find it more helpful and encouraging to literally flip through the pages to look at the beautiful family tree growing. These affirmations and the visual inspiration can help prepare you and at times protect you from the highs and possible low points throughout your journey. There are also affirmations to share with your support system. Encourage them to read and use them as they provide you with loving support. There is even a page for you to add additional affirmations that you yourself create and find helpful throughout your journey.

Above all, we know that as long as you remain hopeful, the right child will find you at the right time. Every part of what happens during your journey can make you stronger, as long as you trust the process. Also, know that when you show the birth mom and child your love, you'll reap immeasurable rewards—whether or not that specific child becomes the one whom you'll raise lovingly forever.

NOTE: *Whenever we use the term "birth mom," it also refers to birth parents if the child's birth father is involved. Throughout affirmations, we use "I," yet we realize that couples may want to use "we" when reading and using the affirmations.*

The Three Most Important Affirmations
For Every Part of My Journey

🍃 I will become an adoptive parent.

🍃 There is a child out there meant for me.

🍃 With hope in my heart, my family tree will grow.

Affirmations for
Choosing to Adopt

There are so many pathways to parenthood. And, there will always be children in need of the love you have to give. Just considering adoption is a beautiful first step. Finalizing that decision in your mind, heart, and soul may come easily or it may take months or even years. It can be the hardest thing you've ever considered. May these affirmations nurture you so that you'll know your answer within your heart.

 Everything I have done in the past and everything I am doing now will lead me to becoming an adoptive parent.

 The right child will find me.

 I know in the deepest part of my being that I am the right parent for the child who is coming to me.

 I am completely worthy to be considered by birth moms.

Affirmations for
Whom to Adopt

Even before learning about the adoption process, most people have thought about "whom" to adopt. By that, we mean what nationality/ethnicity, what gender, what age, and what medical background. While it is so important to be clear on what you want in order to be true to yourself, the more open and flexible you are, the greater the chance the right child will find you more quickly. More often than not, those pursuing adoption end up softening their requirements as they go along. In so doing, they end up finding the child of their dreams.

 My heart is fully open to consider every child who comes my way.

 Every possibility will help lead me to the precious child I will love forever.

 I am flexible. I am loving. I trust my heart. All these qualities within me will lead me to parenthood.

 As I let go of "my list" of who the perfect child is for me, I trust that my child will find the perfect parent in me.

Affirmations for
Choosing My Circle of Support

It is so important to have the right people around you as you pursue adoption: loving people who will carefully listen to you, think and express themselves thoughtfully, cheer you on, and who will hold you up when you need someone to lean on. The right people may be family members, friends, spiritual confidants, or even new people who come into your life when you need them most, such as other adoptive parents. By affirming that you have the right people by your side, you will create for yourself a much more peaceful journey to parenthood.

 I attract only loving and supportive family, friends, and others during my adoption journey.

 Only goodness and kindness from family, friends, and others will guide me.

 I fully trust that my adoption professionals and other resourceful people will help me expand my circle of support.

 I am loved and supported by adoptive parents, adoptees, and others whose lives have been touched by adoption.

Affirmations for
Choosing the Right Adoption Professionals

Equally important as having the right loved ones around you is to have chosen the right adoption professionals to guide you. The right adoption professionals will care deeply about you and your adoption plan. They will keep you on track and make sure every part of the process is done with utmost professionalism and care. Professionals you may be dealing with include: social workers, adoption facilitators, attorneys, and staff at nonprofits and places of worship, among others. Saying these affirmations will put you in the right frame of mind to draw in and work alongside only the right adoption professionals for you. For this reason, it is important to continue to repeat these affirmations throughout every phase of the process.

 I attract the right adoption professionals to help me fulfill my dream of adopting.

 I align myself with adoption professionals who are warm, supportive, available, concerned, and caring.

 I will know I have found the right professionals when they express as much belief as I do that there's a child out there meant just for me.

 I trust that my adoption professionals will be here at the right time to help me.

Affirmations for
My "Emotional Pregnancy"

For many, their pathway to parenthood came after a nine-month physical pregnancy. For us, who have adopted, it was a pregnancy as well . . . an emotional one of the heart, soul, mind, and spirit. We went through labor pains—the labor of hoping, waiting, and believing. We had cravings—to meet the perfect birth mom and to find a healthy child that fit every requirement we came up with. And, while some adoptive parents have a short emotional pregnancy and their child finds them quickly, most journeys go well beyond the nine-month wait. However long your emotional pregnancy, it is so important to affirm your commitment to becoming an adoptive parent and to feel privileged to adopt.

 I embrace every step of the beautiful emotional pregnancy I experience as my baby grows inside his or her birth mom.

 I will become a nurturing parent, through a love-related versus blood-related connection.

 I am fully ready—in my mind, body, and spirit—to begin my path to parenthood through adoption.

I keep a heart full of hope.
My family tree will grow strong.

Affirmations for
My Age

One's age can definitely be a source of doubt. Am I too old to adopt? At my age, will it be fair to my child-to-be? How old will I be when they start school, finish school, get married? Am I thinking more about my needs than that of the baby's/child's? Will I be around long enough to give a child all the love he or she deserves and needs? These are common thoughts, especially if you're past the childbearing age. Adoptive parents are many different ages. And, there are so many grateful adopted children as a result. So to put these kinds of doubts to rest, affirm that you believe in yourself no matter what your age.

 I am the right age to provide a beautiful childhood and loving home for my child.

 This is the right time of my life to welcome my child into my loving family.

 The child I adopt will flourish because of the experience and wisdom I have gained throughout my life.

21

Affirmations for
Being a Single Adoptive Parent

Becoming an adoptive parent, whether you're single or as a couple, is beautiful. Some of you who are single may still be looking for "Mr. or Mrs. Right," yet you know in your heart now is the time to become a parent. Others of you prefer to remain single and also know now is the time to become a parent. Society has come a long way in appreciating all kinds of family units, and you may be lovingly admired by others for your decision to adopt. However, some may try to discourage you—from their own place of fear. Don't let them, especially because you have more than enough love to give your child.

 I am completely capable of and ready to provide a healthy and loving home for my adoptive child. (Add in, "as a single person" if this helps you.)

 I have an abundance of love to give.

 I have enough resources to share.

 I have a good support system to draw upon.

 I am open to finding the right partner, yet I am fully ready now, with open arms, for my adoptive child to find me.

Affirmations for
Handling My Fears

Will I be able to bond? Will the child be able to bond with me? Am I doing the right thing? Can I even afford the adoption process? Will the child be healthy? Will the birth mom like me? Will she choose me? Will she go through with it? Am I ready for all of this?

There are a gazillion questions you will ask yourself now and throughout the process—many of which may come from a place of fear given all the unknowns. The major inspiration for this Adoption Affirmations book was to help you manage your fear throughout the process so you can fulfill your dream of family. As a gift to your future child, promise yourself two things: 1) You will handle your fear, and 2) Giving up on your dream is not an option. Remember, there will be a child out there just for you.

Also realize that whatever fears you are having can be put into perspective with the help of your adoption team, loving personal support system, and through these words and the visual inspiration.

 There is no fear that is larger than the love I have in my heart for the child who is coming.

 I feel and experience the many emotions that come with this journey and keep moving forward toward my beautiful goal of becoming a parent.

 I hear and trust my inner wisdom throughout my journey to parenthood.

 I am human.

 I am optimistic and excited for my dream to be realized.

An adoptive parent is what I am meant to be.

 I will meet my child's emotional, physical, material, and spiritual needs.

 The necessary resources will show up in my life. Financial challenges will melt away.

 My child and I will be love-related instead of blood-related.

 I know deep within my heart the right child will find me and I will find them.

 Giving up is not an option.

Affirmations for
Once a Birth Mom Has Shown Interest

A birth mom has now shown interest in you. This is the moment you've been waiting for. Often, the first reaction you'll have is a feeling of excitement. For some, immediately after, fear or doubt may set in because of all the unknowns. Hopefully you'll remain in a place of strength due to all your positive self-talk. However, whatever you're feeling, remember that your state of mind is so important for you personally and for when you meet the birth mom.

Whether it's the first birth mom or one of possibly the many you'll meet during your journey, most adoptive parents say this is the scariest part of the whole process. Realize it may also be scary for the birth mom. In a sense you're being judged while also seeking to find out if she's the right match for you. You'll want to know everything about the birth mom—most likely first . . . Is she healthy and is her pregnancy going well? You may ask yourself . . . Is this too good to be true? It's also natural to worry about whether or not she'll feel a connection with you.

Though possibly a scary time, it can also be one of the most amazing and precious parts of your entire journey as you get to know one another. Fears can be replaced with clarity and peace of mind for all involved. This birth mom is contemplating giving you the most precious gift—the child she is bearing. So allow your concerns to fade away while you also provide her comfort. Breathe deeply, and then let these affirmations help prepare you for such a beautiful gift of a lifetime.

 I feel the joy of being selected by a birth mom. This is really happening!

 I am in the right place at the right time. I am on the right path.

 I trust the time I invest in being the birth mom's choice is exactly where I am supposed to be in my journey to parenthood.

This moment is mine to celebrate.

 I remain peaceful, hopeful, and compassionate.

 I embrace every opportunity to get to know the birth mom of my child.

 The birth mom and I will move through this journey together with ease.

 I honor the courage it takes to give up one's baby.

 Every birth mom I meet is one step closer to my becoming an adoptive parent.

 I lovingly welcome every birth mom I meet.

 Every birth mom I meet is a gift.

 Humbly, I realize I am a gift for every birth mom I meet.

 I am thankful to be on this journey.

Affirmations for
Enduring the Wait

For some, the journey takes only months. For others, it can take a year or more to find the child who is meant for them. For one of us, it took five years of embracing every new opportunity as if it were the first and each time never giving up hope. The longer the wait, the more important it is to keep affirming your belief in the process, in yourself, and in knowing your child will find you.

While waiting, it might not be as easy for you to see other parents having children. Being invited to and attending their baby showers may also be tough. Coming from and remaining in a place of happiness and joy, however, can be very helpful in your own journey.

Even if a birth mom has shown interest in you, just waiting to hear if she picked you can feel like an eternity. Then once you're chosen, the wait to finally meet your child can also feel like forever. Then there is the wait to finalize the adoption in court. That's why you'll hear people saying, "Adopting a child is not for the faint of heart." However, we promise you, your child is definitely worth the wait. Every second of it. So be patient. That will be one of your many gifts to them.

 However long or short my journey to parenthood is, I know within my heart and soul that it will happen.

 Every day I wait, I am one day closer to becoming a parent. I know this to be true.

 Every baby I see in my daily life reminds me that my child is on his/her way to me.

 This time of waiting is just temporary. It will pass, and my child will find me.

 The pain I feel as I wait is just another way of saying "I love YOU" to my child-to-be.

  I am patient and strong.

As my hope grows,
so too does the
realization
of my family
tree.

29

Affirmations for
Starting Over
(If Adoption Falls Through)

Starting over when a possible adoption seemed to have so much promise is the most difficult and heartbreaking part of adopting. Though some adoptive parents won't experience this, others will. The birth mom may change her mind before she delivers the child or possibly days after you have taken the child home. We share this reality with heavy hearts and given our firsthand experiences. Yet we also know every possible adoption you go through will teach you something incredibly valuable. And every birth mom and child you meet will touch your life forever in beautiful ways you can't even imagine now. You'll touch their lives, too. It's so important for you to understand this and to know a better situation is out there for you.

You must also release any ill feelings and anger toward the birth mom who changed her mind or reclaimed her child. By doing so, you'll make room in your heart to give to your child-to-be. We know only too well how important it will be for you to nurture yourself. You must feel the pain and then consciously let it go. You may find it helpful to pray or hope the best for the child and birth mom—believing deeply that they receive the best of what they need. Then lovingly move on to find the child meant for you.

 Through my constant expressions of kindness, grace, forgiveness, and hope I have touched the life of a birth mom who needed me.

 Everything that is happening now is happening for the ultimate good.

 My obstacles are moving out of my way; my path to parenthood is clear.

 I am at peace with all that has happened, is happening, and will happen.

 Though these times are difficult, they are only a short phase of life.

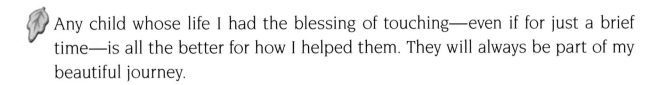 Any child whose life I had the blessing of touching—even if for just a brief time—is all the better for how I helped them. They will always be part of my beautiful journey.

I start today with a pure heart filled with joyfulness and hope to move on.

I thank and peacefully release the birth mom and move on to create my forever family.

Every child I consider has a special space within my heart.

Every child I meet allows my heart to open more for the right child for me.

I now have more proof of my ability to fully love and bond with the child who is meant for me.

Having hope in the birth mom was my way of saying "I love YOU" to my future child.

I continue to forgive and move beyond this to continue my priceless journey to adopt.

I have complete belief and understanding that my child is out there.

My Own
Adoption Affirmations

_____

_____

_____

_____

_____

_____

33

Affirmations for
My Support System to Say to Themselves

We couldn't help but put this section in. As you go through your very personal journey to adopt, your support system (of loved ones, friends, spiritual guides, and others) must be the absolute safest place for you to fully express your doubts, concerns, hopes, and emotions. While they'll have such good intentions, sometimes they may not know how best to say what they feel. Below are several affirmations for *them* to say often to *themselves* to remain in the right frame of mind so you, too, can remain in the right frame of mind through every single step of the process. Please share these with them.

It's important to note that relatives and friends will assume they are within your support system. Everyone you allow in can be a beautiful part of your journey. Yet it will be impossible for them to grasp the full scope of feelings you are going through during this time. It may be one of the most stressful things you've ever gone through, and they may want you to give up because they don't want to see you hurt. They love you. Yet you're strong, and you entered this knowing you'll have no control over when a child will come along, how the birth mom will behave, nor the myriad of other unknowns. What you do have total control over, however, is how you navigate the process and your attitude.

As you believe the right child will find you and you'll find the right child, it's imperative that your support system possess that SAME KIND OF optimism and hope while being completely non-judgemental. Be sure to sit down with your support system and encourage them to say these affirmations to themselves often as a gift to you, to the baby/child that is coming your way, and as a gift to themselves.

I am a constant source of peace, comfort, love, kindness, and hope.

 I express sincerity, honesty, and reliability always.

 I fully trust and respect my loved one(s).

 My words and actions are for the greater good.

 As I come from a place of loving concern, I fully support whatever my loved one(s) decide.

 All these qualities within me will help lead my loved one(s) to adopting.

Affirmations from
My Baby/Child-to-Be

There is one last thought we need to convey . . . and you really need to know. From meeting so many adoptive children and hearing them talk about their adoptive parents, we feel a need to let you know what your baby/child will most likely feel, and may even one day say to you. May these thoughts be inspiration enough for you to always stay steadfast on becoming an adoptive parent.

 I know you dreamed of me. I dreamed of you, too.

 I know you chose me. I chose you, too.

 Thank you for finding me, taking a chance on me, and trusting I would love you.

 I love you forever.

Because I always
had hope . . .

I *now* have
you to love.

37

About the Co-Authors

Keri Gee Semmelman is the lucky mom of a bubbly daughter whom she and her husband adopted at birth. Prior to adopting such a miracle baby (as she weighed only 1½ pounds), they endured a five-year journey that included a couple of adoptions that fell through and numerous other hopefuls. Yet, every experience was meaningful beyond words. In addition to being a doting mom, Keri Gee does community relations work and is an award-winning speaker and presentation trainer, as well as a happiness historian and poet. She has taught on college campuses and actively served on numerous nonprofit boards revolving around helping families and keeping children safe. Her work has led to earning a commendation from former First Lady Barbara Bush and receiving many other distinguished honors. In addition to this book, *Adoption Affirmations*, several others are in the works. She and her family reside in Orange County, California.

Nikki Biers was already a wife and the mother of four children when she became passionate about adopting. She first worked in the field of adoptions in 1991 at an adoption law firm. After remarrying, she did an extensive four years of study to help those in need—both spiritually and physically—which included advocating for pregnant mothers. During that time, she and her husband became adoptive parents, and they opened The Best Gift Adoptions as registered adoption facilitators. During their journey, their second attempted adoption involved the heartbreak of a birth mom reclaiming the baby. Sadly, the child died two weeks later. Never giving up hope and always an inspiration, they went on to fulfill their family tree. This is Nikki's second book. First, she authored a step-by-step information-packed book called *Adoption: The Best Gift—A handbook for prospective adoptive parents*. Highly respected in the field, she has assisted in more than 600 successful adoptions and been featured on radio. She and her family reside in California's San Fernando Valley.

Printed in the United States
By Bookmasters